W9-CDJ-553

Lovingly dedicated to the
special grandmothers in my life:

Mabel Elin Erickson Cowdrick (1909–1988), *I'm glad we got to spend more time with you after you moved to Texas when you became a widow. Your cheerful attitude and independence always impressed me.*

Esther Victoria Elizabeth Gustafson Seiler (1907–1989), *I'll always remember how you hand-squeezed the orange juice for our breakfasts. You were such a gracious hostess.*

Helen Bentsen Brunvoll (1907–1997), *I'm so lucky to have enjoyed you as my own grandmother since marrying your grandson. Your generous love for family will never be forgotten.*

Lydia Olsen Larsen (1910–1987), *How I wish I could have known you. Your delicious waffle recipe is still in use.*

All My Good Habits I Learned from Grandma
Copyright © 2007 by Laurel Seiler Brunvoll

Published in Nashville, Tennessee, by Thomas Nelson, Inc.

Published in association with William K. Jensen Literary Agency, Eugene, Oregon.

Project Editor: Lisa Stilwell

Designed by Greg Jackson, Thinkpen Design, LLC.

ISBN-10: 1-4041-0444-5
ISBN-13: 978-1-4041-0444-0

Printed and bound in the United States of America

ALL MY GOOD HABITS I LEARNED FROM GRANDMA

LAUREL SEILER BRUNVOLL

THOMAS NELSON
Since 1798

NASHVILLE DALLAS MEXICO CITY RIO DE JANEIRO BEIJING

Table of Contents

“If you don’t stand for something, you will fall for anything.”

A mother becomes a true grandmother
the day she stops noticing the terrible things
her children do because she is so enchanted with
the wonderful things her grandchildren do.

LOIS WYSE

That's What Grandmothers Are For

BY ARLENE USLANDER

Most grandmothers are unbelievably loving, patient, and forgiving—and they can think up more excuses for their grandchildren's misbehavior than even those grandchildren can.

When one of my children is cranky (I prefer the word *cranky* to *obnoxious*), Grandma can always be depended on to come up with the reason: "His mattress is too soft; he didn't get a good night's sleep last night." "He's suffering from indigestion from your cooking." "The poor child had to take out the garbage in the rain. Now he's on the verge of pneumonia."

If one of my sons gets into a fight with a child in the neighborhood, it was, of course, the other child's fault. The fact that the alleged bully may have been four years younger and twenty-five pounds lighter than the "innocent victim" has no possible bearing on the case.

When my boys fight with each other and one gets whacked over the head with a tennis racket, it was an accident. "I know you didn't hurt your brother on purpose," Grandma comforts the culprit.

"You're right," he says, nestling against Grandma's comfortable shoulder. "I must need glasses. Your other grandson's head looked just like a tennis ball."

When the boys play the piano, only a grandmother would close her eyes, sigh, and make the unbiased observation: "Ah, Beethoven lives again!"

"They made quite a few mistakes because they didn't practice enough," I point out.

"Don't be silly," says Grandma. "Your piano needs tuning!"

Grandma gave my older son his first baseball uniform—when he was still wearing diapers. So, naturally, she takes great pride in his athletic career and goes to all his games. When the star player of the junior-high set strikes out, it's because "the sun was in his eyes." When he's called out at home plate, it's because "he was tripped on the way." If he misses a ball—well, he just couldn't reach it because "his pants were too tight." (Maybe he could use a new uniform, Grandma!)

When the children recite off-color limericks at the dinner table instead of eating, they have "creative minds."

When they decorate their bedroom walls with charcoal sketches made from ashes in the fireplace, they have "artistic souls."

But I seem to recall that, when I misbehaved as a youngster, my children's grandmother offered only one explanation: "She's just a miserable kid!" ❊

"Good things come to those who wait."

When a child is born,
so are grandmothers.

JUDITH LEVY

With Eyes Wide Open

BY HANNAH MARIE ROOP

She happily marched along the crowded path of the amusement park, under the overhanging trees, between food stands, and around game booths. She was very sure of her destination. She avoided little kids having a meltdown in the summer heat, and she walked past all the other rides. Who was this sure-footed person? It was my nearly seventy-year-old grandma!

There she was, proudly leading my cousins and me to what I thought was our certain doom. The great roller coaster that stood before us was the largest one I had ever seen. I hadn't been very fond of roller coasters in the past, but this time I was determined to overcome my fear and go. My grandma waved us toward the line of nervous people.

"Are you sure you want to do this?" my cousin turned and asked me.

I wasn't really sure, but since I was known for being daring, I squeaked out a soft "yeah."

We caught up to my grandma, and she announced, "Good! The line isn't long!"

I found myself wishing it were. We all leaned up against the plastic fence that was guiding the line. I briefly looked over it to a flume ride with only one little hill. *That's more my speed*, I thought, making a mental note to go on it to calm myself down after this monster roller coaster.

My mom, who tried to comfort us, said, "It's okay to scream. Screaming makes you less scared."

I barely heard what she said. I kept looking up at the ride and cringing at the terrified screams of the riders.

"Great Bear is my favorite ride," my grandma told us with childlike excitement. "It's smooth and a lot of fun!"

I wasn't so sure. While watching it, I had seen the amazing skyscraper-high slopes—at least they seemed that high to me. I had also heard the screaming and the roar of the Great Bear roller coaster. The thick metal tubes didn't seem strong enough to hold the dangling purple cars filled with people.

"Do you want to sit with me?" my grandma offered.

"Yes," I quickly answered and took her hand like an obedient little child.

Everything seemed to move in slow motion as we crept closer and closer to the front of the line. Finally, it was our turn! We buckled our seatbelts as the announcer reminded us of the sixty-one miles per hour speed and the 124-foot drop. I felt so numb I could hardly tell we were moving. My dangling legs didn't help my nervousness.

My grandma was excited and told me not to worry. I closed my eyes and off we went. The ride started with us going down a small hill. Relieved, I opened my eyes—only to find myself hanging high above the park! As we descended the menacing drop, I shut my eyes and screamed.

I kept my eyes closed for the entire ride. I felt the corkscrew loops, the sudden twists, and the unexpected drops. Then, when I felt the car slowing down, I cautiously opened my eyes. The ride was over!

"That was it?" I wondered.

My grandma laughed and said, "That was it!"

I felt as if I had missed out on the ride. "Let's go again!" I said as we left.

My mom was not as enthusiastic. "I don't know. Maybe we should give Grandma a rest—"

My grandma interrupted. "Oh no! I'm fine, Donna."

"Cool!" I shouted.

My mom and my aunt backed out of the next ride with comments about nausea and mutterings of regret. My grandma and I went again. I went through the same nervous symptoms, but I kept my eyes open this time and enjoyed the ride twice as much. Afterward, my grandma led us through the rest of Hershey Park, telling us about how the Super Duper Looper was the first metal roller coaster in Hershey Park, and my parents added how in its day this ride had been, as the Great Bear was now, the scariest ride in the park.

From the Wild Mouse to the Comet, my grandma rode every ride that we did, even when my parents had to skip out. My grandma approaches life the same way she tackled Hershey Park. Day by day and step by step, she does all she can for other people—and she does so wholeheartedly. She does these things even when she can't see where life is taking her, like when we were riding on the Great Bear and couldn't see the track. Grandma taught me not to be afraid and to ride through life with my eyes open. ❊

“Never make a promise you can’t keep.”

I don't intentionally spoil my grandkids.
It's just that correcting them often
takes more energy than I have left.

GENE PERRET

Grandma's Love and Discipline

BY ROBIN BRYCE

Backing up slowly and steadily, easing toward my escape route, I reached the edge of the dining room with my eyebrows almost on the top of my head, my eyes as big as Moon Pies, and my jaw gaping open. I was amazed and somewhat frightened, because this was the first time I had ever seen her this way. She was ruffled—and unraveling fast.

"She" was my grandmother, a somewhat stoic, routinely steady, nothing-ruffles-my-feathers kind of lady. She possessed fair skin, aging strawberry-brown hair, a pudgy body, and a serious face that often wore a smile. And she had survived the Great Depression and all of life's tragedies because of her strong faith in God. She was the backbone and pillar of faith in our family.

My brothers and I regularly spent part of our summer vacation with our grandparents, becoming a part of their home during those weeks. We had regularly scheduled chores, meals, and bedtimes. We were trained to help around the house, and we passed part of the time hanging the laundry or doing other around-the-house activities with Grandma.

Our grandma didn't play much, but she would tell us interesting stories about our ancestors and use picture albums to illustrate each one. In the rest of our time, we would amuse ourselves climbing Grandma's pear trees, building miniature boats in our grandfather's workshop and then floating them in the creek, or finding some other mischief. I can still hear Grandma hollering, "Get down out of that tree before you break off my bearing branches!" Other times she would warn, "Get out of that creek! Don't you get wet—and watch out for snakes!"

Most of the time, my brothers and I stumbled into trouble; we weren't really seeking it. And sometimes trouble just found us. But back to my grandma's undoing. Exactly what my brother's violation was—and whether I had a part in it—has long escaped my memory. How Grandma found him out is an uncertainty as well. As young children, we innocently could have told her. I'm guessing, though, that I probably squealed since I liked it when my brother Keith got into trouble.

But this unraveling of my grandma was an awe-inspiring sight. She stood in the middle of the room, her fair face turning redder by the second. Her arms were planted firmly onto her hips, and steam began pouring out of her mouth in short bursts. "Come here to me!...What did you do?...Why did you do that?...

I said, 'Come...here...to...me!!" That last sentence slowed as she emphasized every word.

I had seen mothers act like this plenty of times and had never been very concerned. But this was Grandma! As she said, "Come," I scooted away as inconspicuously as possible while Grandma focused on the little culprit across the room.

Keith found himself up against a proverbial wall. The dining table was also pushed up against the wall—literally. Chairs were properly pushed under at their assigned spots. Weaving in and out, over and under the maze of wooden table legs and chair legs—and always under the protection of the tabletop—was my brother.

Astonished and actually quite frightened by Keith's actions as well as Grandma's, I covered my small tale-telling mouth with both hands.

Grandma ran back and forth from one end of the table to the other, spitting and sputtering as she went, while Jack Be Nimble quickly and skillfully maneuvered around under the table.

I have to admit that, as I realized Keith had Grandma beat, the covering of my mouth began to serve a different purpose. My hands now covered a smile that quickly turned into a stifled chuckle. Still trying to blend into the wallpaper and not draw attention to myself, I saw Keith starting to smile as he noticed the success of his getaway plan.

Unsure about Grandma's next move, though, Keith kept the chase going, back and forth, going to one end of the table and then to the other. This dance grew more and more comical, but we weren't at all sure if Grandma was amused. So we held our amusement to a grin.

Grandma began to tire, and her fair face became flush with exercise instead of anger. The steam of her temper had evaporated. She must have seen Keith's grin or a glimpse of mine, because she burst out giggling. "Oh, come on out of there. I can't spank you now. I'm too winded." Laughing again, she added, "I will tell your parents, though."

We all laughed, giggled, and hugged. We told Grandma we were sorry for whatever it was we had done wrong, but we did think the discipline was a tremendously fun activity. In fact, we begged to do it again.

I pleaded, "Yeah! And this time I want to be the one under the table."

Grandma did tell our parents about our infraction, but she went straight into defending us and wouldn't hear of any further discipline. She stated that we had learned our lesson and had promised not to disobey her again. And that's how I learned that discipline has much to do with relationships.

So, whenever I find myself spitting and sputtering with steam, I step back and find some humor in it. Laughter restores, cheers, and lifts me above many undesirable situations. We can more easily endure life's toughest spots by laughing at our mistakes and at ourselves. Our perspective on life changes, and laughter becomes much better than medicine.

Grandma's laughter is a good habit. Just like her discipline. ❊

Grandmas hold our tiny hands for just a little while, but our hearts forever.

AUTHOR UNKNOWN

Baby Blessings

BY SARAH ELAINE SIMS

At 2:30 a.m. on this muggy August night, the Oklahoma truck stop bustled with bleary-eyed drivers and slinking teenagers roaring in and out of the parking lot. I was struggling to nurse my twelve-week-old daughter in the back of my parents' Ford Windstar while my dad paced around the gas pumps. Having to stop every two hours to feed or change the baby, we were not making good time. My mom would doze off between her anxious calls to the backseat, "Are you doing okay?"

The four of us were on our way to a family reunion. My parents had been surprised that I wanted to accompany them on what should have been a six-hour drive. After all, my husband couldn't get off work to join us, and there would always be another family reunion in a year or so. Traveling with my first baby sounded laborious at best, especially since I was a brand-new mom, but something told me that I needed to go along.

In the bleak darkness we drove into the plains of southern Kansas where my grandparents had raised cattle during the 1930s and '40s. I thought such a life must have been as dry and cheerless as the rain-starved fields. The few photographs I could recall of my dad's family when the kids were young reveal my wiry grandmother with her tight-set lips surrounded by her eleven children, ages four to thirty. Both she and my grandfather sternly peered straight ahead, as if they needed to get back to milking the cows and could not abide this fool picture-taking.

My grandmother, now widowed more than twenty years and well into her eighties, lived alone only a few scant miles from where she had been born. She still milked the cow every day and raised her own chickens. She was the reason I traveled that night.

In her car seat Baby Abigail struggled not to fall asleep, and I prayed we wouldn't have to stop again. I stroked her downy head and tried to close my eyes. As I dozed, I longed to see the dirt driveway leading up to the little green farmhouse nestled in the trees along Big Sandy Creek. And with a tired sigh, I reminisced.

Grown-ups would catch up on news while leaning against a pickup in the dark shade of the oak tree. They would laugh together over the clatter of the pots and pans in Grandma's kitchen. When it was time for dinner, a line of aunts, uncles, and cousins wound through the kitchen, past the laundry area, off the porch, and out the door.

The smell of roast beef and mashed potatoes whetted our appetite as we laughed and teased one another. The summer heat could only be relieved by the deep shade of the cottonwoods and the iced tea dipped out of a bucket. Desserts of frosted cookies, brownies, and angel food cake—all laid out on the washer and dryer—would tempt us as we waited our turn to load our plates.

As the afternoon wore on, there would be hand-cranked vanilla ice cream doled out in teal plastic teacups. The grown-ups would squeeze around the kitchen table, their chair backs pressed up against the walls, but everyone under thirty would find a cousin or two and sit on the stairs, in rocking recliners, outside on metal lawn chairs near the storm cellar, in any clear spot they could find.

The screen door would screech open and bang shut again and again as the grandkids ran in and out to play. The boys would dash into the woods behind the house or down the ravine to splash in the creek and catch turtles and frogs. The girls would eat mulberries and climb to the top of the big, white hay barn in search of the latest litter of kittens.

The boys would hunt water moccasins and copperheads. There was always a snake sighting somewhere—one time in Grandma's living room. And she chopped the head right off a four-foot snake as all the nearby grandchildren gathered around in a half circle of gory admiration!

We arrived at my uncle's motel around 4:00 a.m. We planned to sleep a little before traveling the short distance to the farm, but as soon as we lay down, we were awakened by a knock at the door. I had slept in my clothes, so I stumbled to the door in the darkness. Baby Abigail stirred and made a little cry.

I heard my mom's voice: "Sarah, open the door."

The bright Kansas sunlight poured into the tiny room. The heavy draperies had kept the room so dark, I had not yet realized it was full day.

My grandmother's slight figure and tight-lipped smile greeted me. A hard life on the farm had robbed her of an easy smile and generous laughter. Her brown eyes revealed her delight, however. I embraced her warmly as her thin, strong arms enveloped me.

I was never quite sure why she had come to town that morning, but my guess is that she wanted to see my baby daughter before more than sixty of my grandmother's children, grandchildren, and great-grandchildren crowded together for the last reunion at the farm. The next reunion, and all those that followed, would be very different. My grandmother's mental health would deteriorate to the point where recognizing her numerous family members proved to be too much.

But right now, for these few quiet moments in our motel room, Grandma could be alone with my new baby and me. She sat down on the bed and lifted the tiny figure gently onto her lap. I hadn't yet dressed my baby in her new pink romper with the delicate embroidery. She didn't yet have the satin hair bow or her brown curls pressed into place. Abigail was still in her pajamas and not the least bit ready to meet her great-grandmother for the first time.

Even so, this grandmother of thirty-six and great-grandmother of forty gazed tenderly into Abigail's big blue eyes as if Abigail were the precious firstborn grandchild.

"What's her name?" Grandma's question revealed the enormity of her brood, but she continued to take in every move and sound Abigail made, savoring her kicks and waves.

"Abigail Elizabeth," I said, standing back a little and feeling just a bit nervous.

"Pretty name." Grandma's simple pronouncement meant approval.

A stream of sunlight highlighted the two as they sat on the bed. Grandma held Abigail close to her face for a moment, lightly touching her cheek to the baby's. The only sounds were Abigail's soft baby gurgles and coos.

"I always did love babies," Grandma said, her voice rich and full. Her eyes shone with joy as she smiled a rare smile at Abigail's baby grin.

"Me too, Grandma," I whispered. ❄

Grandparents are similar to a piece of string—handy to have around, and easily wrapped around the fingers of their grandchildren.

AUTHOR UNKNOWN

Every Little Stitch

BY LORETTA CAMPBELL

My grandmother was inseparable from her sewing machine. Born in 1914, Phyllis Marie taught herself her to sew, and as a teenager she got a job making men's shirts at a local factory. Once she became a wife and mother, she quit work, but she did sew at home for her family. She made everything from baby clothes to suits, from napkins to curtains, with nothing but a measuring tape and a talented eye. Rarely did she ever buy precut patterns. She raised four children, and as they grew, her sewing machine turned out prom clothes, graduation gowns, and all seven bridesmaid dresses for an elaborate wedding. Time went by quickly, and before Phyllis knew it, she was making baby clothes again—this time, as a grandmother.

When I was a little girl, I loved going to Grandma's house. The sewing machine was always whirring happily, and whenever I hear that sound today, I can't help but think of her. She made blankets and clothes for all eight of her grandchildren and twelve great-grandchildren, and she continued to fill the homes of her adult children with essentials like potholders and tea cozies.

All of us grandchildren agree, however, that her best sewing was when she made clothes for our many dolls and stuffed toys. Every summer Grandma came with her tape measure and carefully took the measurements of our dolls' legs, arms, and bodies. Then she would create the most amazing wardrobes for them—and I'm not talking about a few dresses. She made coats with bonnets, pants and shirts, dresses with matching bloomers, nightgowns, and bathrobes. She created every outfit a pampered doll could possibly dream of—and more! As if sheer quantity and variety were not impressive enough, every outfit also came adorned with pockets, buttons, lace, and ruffles. She added intricate details that were precious to us, even as children, and they clearly showed the love and dedication she poured into her sewing.

The boys were not left out either. Grandma created fantastic wardrobes for their stuffed animals—military uniforms, three-piece tuxedos, farmer overalls, and more. She made everything a manly teddy bear could need, complete with hats, belts, and badges. She even had a slot in the back for the tail to poke through. The boys loved their animal wardrobes as much as we girls treasured our dolls'. Every pocket, every button, and every touch of rickrack showed us how much Grandma cared.

Phyllis Marie passed away the same week of her ninetieth birthday. During the memorial service, the church was packed full of people who loved and remembered her. As they both grieved and celebrated her life, every person had a story to tell about something she had once sewn for them.

It's a tragedy that no one in our family has taken her place. But since she was such a talented seamstress, none of her four children—or sixteen grandchildren—ever needed to learn how to sew. So now, for the first time, her sewing machine sits silently beneath a vinyl cover. She left behind twenty-two great-grandchildren. Who will sew for them? Indeed, a great art has been lost for much of society. There are still some seamstresses and tailors in this world, but far more people think that clothing and potholders only come from a factory.

The cardboard box full of old doll clothes that I saved from my childhood is tattered and falling apart, but the clothes within it are as sturdy as ever. The buttons are tight, and the seams strong, despite countless washings and dressings. I want my children to know that kind of quality, that level of care being invested in one's work. I don't want my children to grow up thinking that life is about getting things fast and cheap. Instead, I want them to know what their great-grandmother taught me—life is about what you put into every little stitch. ❈

“It costs nothing to be kind.”

Grandparents are a delightful blend of laughter, caring deeds, wonderful stories, and love.

AUTHOR UNKNOWN

Gran's Secret

BY MARIANNE CRONE

The rattle of wheels over the cobbled street outside woke Victoria. She cupped her hands over her cold nose—it felt like an icicle. She buried her face in the pink woolen blankets, stretched out her legs, and quickly curled up. The end of the bed was ice-cold.

Gray morning light crept in from under the curtains as Victoria peeped over the blankets. She eyed her family of dolls standing on the balcony of the dollhouse. *A good thing Gran knit them tiny jumpers,* she thought. Through her lashes, Victoria thought the family looked as though they were waving. She waved back.

The rattle grew louder, and milk bottles clattered in their boxes.

"We can't get up yet," she said to Teddy, who gazed back at her with deep, lifeless button eyes. "Gran says when I hear the milkman, it's still too early. We must wait for the horse and the baker."

Victoria loved to sleep in the big bed with the pink blankets and three soft pillows. She fluffed up one of them, sat up, and leaned against it.

"Now look, Teddy," she said as she opened her picture book and pointed at a picture of a cow, "this is an herbivore, and he eats grass."

But Teddy did not giggle. Dad had taught her about herbivores and carnivores. Whenever she used these words, everybody chuckled, but not Teddy.

When they had finished the book, she took Teddy by the arm and went to the window covered with frosty flowers. She traced the contours with her finger and some of the ice melted, but not enough for her to be able to look outside. *Pufff hufff!* Her warm breath made a little hole in the frosty patterns. Craning her neck for a closer look outside, Victoria could just make out the baker's cart and his horse, trotting along the street below.

She hopped from one foot to the other because the linoleum was stone-cold. She found a pair of slippers under the bed and quickly put them on. They were miles too big. Yesterday, when she arrived at Gran's, she realized that she'd forgotten to pack her own. These were much nicer, though, because they were furry inside and tickled her toes.

Back at the window, she pushed Teddy's nose against the frost flowers and whispered something in his ear. She looked Teddy in the eye, said, "It's not scary, you know," and gave him a big hug.

The clip-clop of the horse's hooves was now right under her window. "Let's go!" she said to Teddy and skipped down the stairs, holding on to the banister with one hand and to Teddy with the other, his head hanging down and bumping each step. "Sorry, Teddy," she said. "Hurt?" And she gave him a kiss on his jet-black nose.

She knocked on Gran's door.

"Morning, my princess," Gran said and peeked at her from above the covers with one eye. "Love your slippers."

"They're yours," Victoria said with a smile as she scuffed across the wooden floor. She planted a kiss right on the tip of Gran's nose and sat down on the edge of the bed. "Can I see now?"

Gran nodded, and Victoria made a dash for the dressing table. It was cluttered with little pots of cream, scent bottles, a powder puff, and a big, blue bowl of talcum powder. She propped Teddy against a bottle of eye lotion.

Victoria sat down on the taboret and gave a big sigh of delight.

"Look, Teddy! This is it!" she said as she held her hands behind her back. "And don't you dare touch it!"

Gran smiled.

Victoria looked at it from all sides. "It" was a glass filled with water. When she moved her head up and down, she saw the round object inside change shape. It became longer and thinner. When she moved her head from left to right, it became wide and thin. When she looked at it from the top, it resembled a marble—a big one! But it wasn't round. It was the shape of an egg, but smaller of course. An egg wouldn't fit. It was milky white and had a black dot surrounded by a gray-blue halo.

Gran put on her dressing gown and stood next to Victoria.

"Seen enough, princess?" she asked.

Victoria nodded and got up.

Gran sat down on the stool in front of the dressing table and put the glass in front of her. Victoria watched every single movement. With two fingers, Gran stretched open her closed eyelid. With her right hand she fished the big marble out of the water and held it between her finger and thumb. Slowly she slid the glass eye into the empty socket, and then she blinked.

Now with two gray-blue eyes, Gran turned, looked at Victoria, and said, "Our little secret, my princess." They smiled at each other conspiratorially. ❋

“When you are down to nothing, God is up to something.”

Grandmothers are a special gift to children.

AUTHOR UNKNOWN

Lessons from Grandma's Grocery Store

BY EVA C. MADDOX

I ran full steam ahead toward the old screen door of Grandma's country store. "Gram!" I yelled, letting the door slam behind me as I let myself in.

"I'm right here, Evie. Same as always."

I skipped to the back of the store and saw that Grandma was holding a Mason jar halfway behind her back.

"What's that, Gram?" I asked, pointing to the jar.

She frowned and pushed back the wisps of hair escaping from the little bun on the back of her head.

"Must you be so rambunctious, Evie?" she asked.

"Sorry, Gram. What's in that jar you're holding?"

"Well, I was just about to put a quarter in it when you came storming in."

Clink! went the quarter. Then she held up the jar that was almost filled to the top with coins.

"Gosh, Gram, that's a lot of money!"

"Sssh!" she warned as she placed the jar behind some old crates. "This is a secret between you and me, Evie."

"I won't tell a soul, Gram, but I don't understand why you don't just take your money to the bank."

"I do take most of my money to the bank, but I like seeing how much I can save by just setting aside a few coins each day. Did you see that new rocking chair on my front porch?"

"Uh-huh."

"Well, I paid for it by simply saving quarters, dimes, nickels, and even pennies."

"Wow! That's a great idea, Gram. I'm going to start doing that too."

Grandma then went to the cash register and took out a dime. "Here, Evie. You can start your savings jar with this dime."

I stuffed the dime in my pocket and plopped down in an old wicker chair Grandma put by the pickle barrel. Hot and thirsty, I was hoping she would offer me one of those cool sodas she kept in the Coca-Cola™ case. I knew she was probably saving them for the neighbors who came in to cool off, though. Then I spotted some bottles of root beer on the topmost shelf.

"What kind of root beer is that up there, Gram?" I asked, pointing to the shelf.

She was sweeping the old wooden floor, but she paused to answer me. "It's called Granddad's Old-Fashioned Root Beer."

"Have you ever tasted it?"

"No. Can't say that I have," she said, sweeping all around my chair.

"How do you know it's good enough to sell to your customers if you've never tasted it?"

In response to my question, Grandma propped her broom against the counter and pulled an old step stool over to the root-beer shelf. She hiked up her long dress and retrieved a warm bottle of Granddad's Old-Fashioned Root Beer. My eyes lit up.

She put the bottle in the Dr. Pepper™ cap remover that was nailed to the counter and said, "Maybe you better test this out for me. I sure wouldn't want to be selling root beer that isn't good, now would I?"

I gulped down the warm, sweet liquid and noticed that Grandma had a curious twinkle in her eye as a smile broke across her face.

Today, years later, I am a proud grandma, and I, too, can boast of owning a new rocking chair—paid for with quarters, nickels, and dimes from my own Mason jar. And my refrigerator is never without root beer just in case I have a little visitor who is hot and thirsty. ❊

If God had intended us to follow recipes,
He wouldn't have given us grandmothers.

LINDA HENLEY

Magical Pancakes

BY LAUREL SEILER BRUNVOLL

My husband and I felt a sense of great anticipation as we drove the car up the snow-lined driveway. It seemed as if we'd had more than a week's absence from our home and kids. My father-in-law and mother-in-law had graciously offered to stay at the house and take care of our two sons. Now, after an amazing, fun-filled Caribbean cruise, we were excited to see our boys.

"Looks like they had some snowstorms while we were gone," my husband said, looking around the yard. Even though it was nighttime, we could easily make out the shapes of snow forts, snowmen, and leftover snowballs.

As he carefully stepped out of the car, I nodded in agreement, grabbed one of the smaller suitcases, and headed straight inside. The cold wind whipped around us and practically sliced through the coat I had thrown on for the ride home.

We opened the front door and immediately smelled a familiar favorite smell—Norwegian pancakes. The sweet, buttery aroma had lingered and saturated every room in the house.

"Well, I guess Grandma made the boys lots of pancakes this week," I commented to my husband, who is 100 percent Norwegian. He smiled.

"That's my mom...spoiling her grandkids again," he said. He knew how much Josh and Mike loved those thin pancakes. Ever since they were preschoolers, Josh and Mike talked about Grandma's pancakes being magical because they tasted so good and because Grandma made them with love, just for her grandchildren.

As we walked into the house, I glanced into the cleaned-up kitchen. No pancakes in sight! But I could definitely picture Grandma working in the kitchen every morning this past week while we were gone. She would set her alarm each morning so that she could make the pancakes fresh for Josh and Mike before they went to school.

Grandma donned her turquoise-blue cotton robe and walked downstairs to the kitchen. She pulled out a large mixing bowl and beat the eggs and sugar. She methodically beat the flour and milk, then added the melted butter a little bit at a time.

Now that the kids were older, she usually doubled the recipe and kept two skillets busy at the same time. Her years of practice made for perfectly cooked Norwegian pancakes. But it was a gift of time and effort. The daily pancake production took almost two hours from start to finish.

Josh and Mike raced to the kitchen to see who could eat the most pancakes. After placing two or three thin delicacies on their plates, each of them spooned a bit of granulated sugar over the top and then quickly rolled them up one at a time. It only took three, maybe four bites to devour a single pancake.

The house was dark and silent now. Everyone was already asleep. We crept quietly through the hallway and went into Josh and Mike's bedroom. Not wanting to disturb their sleep, I carefully leaned down to give them each a hug and a kiss. My husband did the same.

Before we left, though, Josh turned over and started mumbling. We moved closer to him to try to hear what he was saying. "I want some more of Grandma's magical pancakes," he muttered. ❆

"Tell the truth and you will never have to remember anything."

Wrinkles should merely indicate where smiles have been.

MARK TWAIN

Keep the Wrinkles Away

BY PAT STOCKETT JOHNSTON

Grandma Ruth resembled a greasy, ghostly mime as she stood up and turned toward me. Suddenly realizing I'd be sharing my double bed with this oily apparition during her visit from Oklahoma made me—her ten-year-old bedmate—squirm. I had watched her put on her nightgown and then sink onto the bench in front of the vanity mirror. She tightly held a white glass jar as she carefully unscrewed its lid. Then she started spreading its gunky contents (at first I thought it was Crisco) all over her face, arms, and legs.

"Grandma, why are you smearing that white stuff all over yourself?" I asked.

"I'm keeping my skin from aging," she replied. "This cold cream works like magic. It keeps the wrinkles away and makes me look younger."

I took a good look. *I don't think so,* I thought.

Grandma's forehead was plowed with wrinkles. Deep creases spread like spider webs from the corners of her eyes. The veins on her hands stood out like water pipes lying along the side of the road, and the flab on her arms shook like a bowlful of JELL-O™ when she brushed her hair. Her upper thighs were rolling mounds of flesh. She kept the appearance of a firm stomach by wearing a thick, elastic girdle. Her whole body could be described as "sagging." I couldn't understand why she didn't find that cream a great disappointment.

One thing was for sure, though. My grandma never disappointed me. In fact, I was confident that she loved me better than my five siblings. As an adult, I discovered all six of us shared the same certainty of being her favorite grandchild. What a gift she gave us—the gift of feeling special, of being important, of being worthy of attention. She never criticized us or withheld her love no matter what kind of crazy trouble we got into. Quiet words of comfort and encouragement were all we heard from her lips.

When my husband and I went to Beirut as missionaries, it was Grandma Ruth who wrote regularly. Her letters often described her garden, how many jars of this or that she had canned, and her lunch dates with friends. Those letters all ended with her assurance that she was praying for my safety and my ministry. Knowing my grandma prayed for me helped calm my fears as I adjusted to living in a land fraught with violence.

Long before my own six grandchildren were born, I committed myself to matching my grandma's grandmotherly graces—to loving my grandchildren so fervently that they would always feel my acceptance and want me to visit. I purposed to find time to be alone with each grandchild when we visit his or her home—and that's not always easy since we adults have lots to talk about. I confirm my interest in my grandkids when I read their school reports, listen to their creative-writing stories, and help them with their math. Other activities include playing table games with them, listening to their musical-instrument recital pieces, and encouraging participation in sing-alongs around the piano or with karaoke CDs. Reading to them brings joy to my heart. Because of my grandma Ruth's example, I do all I can to leave a legacy of love with each grandchild. That includes letting them know I pray for them.

Now about that cold cream. A woman of my age should know better than to believe in magical, anti-aging products. However, I'm sure Grandma Ruth is smiling down on me each evening as I apply—not cold cream—but a less-greasy anti-aging ointment called a "moisturizer." As for the presence of flab on my arms and thighs and wrinkles on my brow? Don't even ask. ❋

“When you’re out; be careful.”

It is as grandmothers that our mothers
come into the fullness of their grace.

CHRISTOPHER MORLEY

The Front Porch

BY JANET WARD HOOPES

The tree-lined streets in my grandmother's quiet neighborhood featured miles of sidewalks. These cement paths didn't just border yard and roads; they connected people to one another. In our small Ohio town, your porch was an extension of your home and your heart. Neighborhoods felt safe, families were intact, and front porches were open venues for conversations among neighbors and friends. Growing up in the 1950s, I look back on those fond memories of my grandmother's home and her front porch.

You see, Grandma's front porch was an extension of her enthusiasm for life. We would sit on her big, covered porch—white with a gray wooden plank floor—in either the glider or one of her big, comfortable cushioned chairs. There were a few times she even let me sit in "her" chair, the one closest to the door.

I did a lot of growing up when I was sitting on my grandmother's porch. We'd not only talk about life, but we'd watch life as it walked by on the sidewalk in front of us. I watched my grandma invite everyone who walked by to stop and chat. She frequently offered them a glass of lemonade and a homemade peanut-butter cookie. Kids were included in the conversations, or else they amused themselves with playing jacks, cops and robbers, or hopscotch on the sidewalk. As we got older, we read out on the porch.

By the time my twin brother and I were old enough to remember spending time with her, my grandmother was a widow and had also lost her youngest son in the war. My dad, her second-oldest son, took care of her whenever she needed extra help. She had many friends and was very involved in her church.

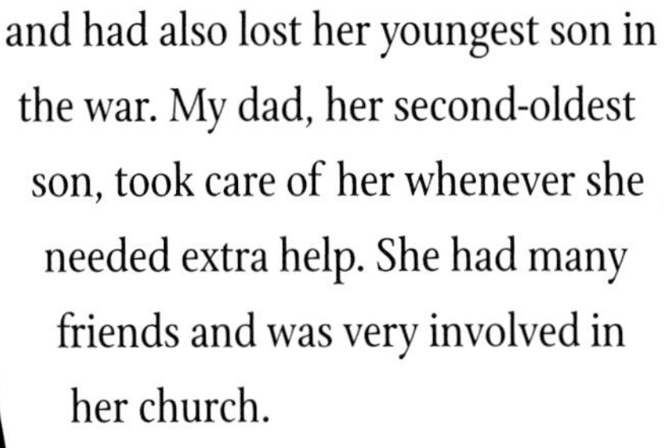

We were the only grandchildren living nearby, and she doted on us. We had open lunches in elementary school, so my brother and I often walked to her house for lunch. I don't remember what we ate. Just spending time with my grandmother in her big, warm kitchen was precious.

It was in that kitchen that she taught me how to bake those delicious peanut-butter cookies and put the fork-tine indentations on them. She would also fry what we termed "rubber bacon" for Jim and me. And it was in her kitchen that she gleefully set out the Monopoly board. She couldn't wait to get all those hotels and beat the pants off us. We weren't allowed to quit until the game was won. I really don't remember ever winning, but playing the game with her was endearing and sometimes downright exhausting.

My grandmother's joy in life touched me in places I didn't understand when I was a child. I have never forgotten how she always had her Bible open beside her chair, and I knew she read it every day. She underlined it and wrote notes in it—a habit that I gratefully have copied. I now know her strength came from the Lord.

At that time I only knew that my friend Jesus was her friend too. Once in Sunday school I made a stained-glass picture of the Virgin Mary, and she put it up on her wall, where it remained for years. Grandma sent me my first-ever corsage for Easter one year, and she took me for my first manicure. Years later, it dawned on me that she had beautifully manicured nails on her one beautiful hand. My grandmother was born with only one arm; the other ended at her elbow. I hardly noticed that as a child. It certainly never slowed her down in doing anything she chose to do. That loving hand wrote me letters all through my college years.

She did surprise us at times, though. One night my brother Jim and I were spending the night with Grandma. I loved spending the night at her house because I got to sleep in her big bed, and Jim had to sleep on the couch. After we played our usual game of Monopoly, she turned on the television. Apparently it was time for her special show—and little did we know that it would turn out to be wrestling! My grandmother, who seemed old but ageless to me, sat down in her special chair and suddenly starting whooping and yelling at these half-dressed men throwing each other around in the ring!

I was stunned. Watching silently, I remained speechless as she and my brother Jim hooted and hollered. I couldn't wait to tell my dad what his mom watched on television! Even after my dad explained to us what wrestling was all about, my brother and I were never able to convince Grandma that the fights were rigged and that they weren't really hurting each other like it appeared. Knowing my grandmother, maybe it was her joke on us. Clearly, she thoroughly enjoyed those wrestling matches.

After that introduction to wrestling, though, I saw my grandmother in a different light. Now I could see a twinkle in her eye and the sheer joy she experienced in all she did. Most of all, I loved watching my grandmother enjoy herself. She'd often go into the backyard and cut fresh flowers from her beautiful garden. Then she sat on her porch, waiting to give them to her friends as they walked by. I observed many things and learned about life on that front porch. One lesson I've never forgotten is that a life shared brings joy—not only to you but also to others. ❊

"Don't forget to always wear clean underwear."

If becoming a grandmother was only a matter of choice, I should advise every one of you straight away to become one. There is no fun for old people like it!

HANNAH WHITHALL SMITH

Teatime with Bammy

BY LAURIE EPPS

My grandmother was a very typical grandmother in many ways. What set her apart, though, was her insistence in being called "Bammy." She wasn't a Grandma, Nana, or Granny. And there's a reason she was Bammy. My father couldn't pronounce "Granny" when he was a toddler, and it came out "Bammy." My grandmother thought it was so cute that she swore she'd be Bammy when her time came.

My grandmother was always a lady—not only in beauty but also in her demeanor. Every hair on my grandmother's head was always in place. Her dresses were typically long. Of course, her pantsuits were perfectly color coordinated. Her favorite color was dusty rose—and so was mine. She was very soft-spoken, demure, and kind. Bammy often gave compliments, and she usually had some candies to share. Looking back, I will always remember her bright blue eyes reaching out to me over one of her candy dishes.

A trip to see Bammy and Grandfather usually started on a Friday afternoon. Dad got off work early to come home and pack us kids and all our stuff into the family car. We began our five-hour journey north to their little town in South Carolina. This made our arrival quite late. The average time was midnight, but it suited my parents since we'd sleep most of the way. I can still feel my daddy carrying me into the house; I felt as if I were floating on a cloud.

Waking up in the grand old house was special. This house was simple but elegant. Every inch oozed decorum and taste; the house definitely reflected the personality of our Bammy. Outside the house was an old oak tree with Spanish moss hanging from its branches. This combination of antebellum and colonial architecture made it seem as if we had walked onto the set of *Gone with the Wind*.

I loved to wake up and hear my grandfather making breakfast. After breakfast, I'd read a book and imagine I was on an old southern plantation. My grandparents even kept my dad's and aunt's old toys in the upstairs bedrooms. My brother and I would tirelessly play with the goofy, old toys. Usually Grandfather would take my brother out fishing. I actually preferred that so I could have the toys to myself!

Sometime in the early afternoon my mother would call me downstairs. I never did make it all the way downstairs before I heard the formal announcement that Bammy requested the honor of my presence at tea.

After a huge introduction by my mother—as though I were a guest at a garden social—she would exclaim, "But not like that!

You'll have to change into suitable attire!" My reaction varied through time. When I was four to seven years old, I was happy to change. After all, I was a princess. Once I got a little older, though, I'd complain: "Not the itchy tights again! I hate them!" Yet, after a little coercion, I'd always be ready for sweets and tea.

Tea was always at three o'clock. That's the proper time for tea. Anyway, that's what Bammy always said. And tea was held in the most appropriate room in the grand old house—its elegant parlor. Every piece of mahogany or cherrywood furniture had been polished until it shone. All the seat covers were exquisitely detailed and perfectly coordinated with the walls. Every item in the feminine room was dusty rose or a complement. Its European style seemed regal to me, and as soon as I entered the doors, I knew it was time to behave.

Bammy had lots of pretty teapots, teacups, and matching saucers set around the room. Most of them were accented in the warm dusty-rose color. She also had many pretty knickknacks about, which I'm sure required a lot of dusting. The ones that were not tea accessories were usually figurines of either teenage girls in flowing gowns or birds. I was not allowed to touch them without the aid of an adult, so I also didn't need reminding when I went into stores that had breakables.

In the early years of our tea, Bammy made all kinds of sweet treats. I just loved the little cakes and cookies. I especially liked marzipan, tea cakes, and shortbread cookies. As she got older, I did notice that some inferior store-bought cookies took their place. To this day, one bite of the inferior cookies from the grocery store brings back the memory of those tea parties.

However, the menu was incidental to the real purpose of tea. You see, my Bammy used our teatime to both find out about my life and teach me some manners. I learned the proper way to pour and serve the tea. I learned about needlecrafts and how to write thank-you notes. Most of all, she made me feel like I was worth listening to. While my mother got preoccupied with my posture, Bammy would really listen to what I was saying.

Nothing beats those memories of our teas in the grand old house's parlor. ❊

"You never know until you've tried."

There's no place like home
except Grandma's.

AUTHOR UNKNOWN

Iris Waits

BY KATRINA DE MAN

Iris waited at the counter and rubbed her hands at the flour that remained on the wooden cutting board. Standing on the worn patch of hardwood floor in front of the sink, Grammy moved pans and bowls and sorted them into piles. One at a time she'd wash, rinse, and dry a pan and then slowly lean down to put it into the cupboard, her hips spreading out around her as she bent over.

Grammy was fleshy and wrinkled; deep, strong lines ran across her face and through her arms. Her legs had bulgy masses under the dark hose she wore, and her bald head was nicely tucked under a white, curled wig. The wig was sometimes off kilter, and that is how Iris had found out about the baldness.

Grammy's hands were thick and stiff, bumpy-knuckled and clumsy looking, but that didn't slow her down. Whenever she came to visit, Iris saw those hands in constant motion as she worked around the house and helped with all manner of chores.

Iris loved watching her great-grandma cook. Comfortable with her memory, Grammy didn't use recipes; she trusted her careful and knowing hands. Iris' mother tried to follow her around in the kitchen and write down the ingredients, and Grammy would smile and laugh richly and deeply: "Now, dear, don't be too sure of my doings. I never am too certain." But the food was always light and perfect and delicious.

Today Iris was alone in the kitchen with Grammy. With her mother and sisters on a visit to town, the chatter of other mornings was missing. A pleasant shyness drifted around the kitchen as they worked until Iris gathered up her courage and tumbled out the question of how Grammy learned to make the pigs in a blanket they were having for lunch. Grammy told Iris about her mother and the kitchen she grew up in, and Iris stayed quiet, taking in every word. No other person was hearing this story; it was Iris's alone.

As Grammy reminisced, she and Iris mixed the sausage with seasonings and then worked it into small, long rolls. Iris looked on while Grammy mixed flour and water and lard, her fingers testing the damp, clingy combination of ingredients. And then Iris sat at the counter and waited. Grammy had told her to sit down so she could roll out the dough and cut rectangles that would wrap around the sausages like a blanket.

Later, after the dishes were done and the kitchen clean, a fragrance filled the kitchen and Grammy walked over to the stove. Iris watched the tray of crusty, golden treats come out of the oven. Her heart warmed with the thought of how good those blanketed piggies tasted. Grammy patted the rolls and pushed down a little to check for doneness.

Looking out the window, Grammy strained forward and looked all around. As she did so, her hair pushed against the window and then against the cupboard. Unconsciously touching her wig, she turned back to Iris with a smile.

"Well, sis, the pigs are done, and I'm not seeing anyone else around to eat right now. Bring me the plates," Grammy suggested. "I just don't believe these piggies should wait for the others, do you?"

Iris was surprised. Grammy was a stickler about sneaking food before a meal, and now the two of them were going to eat without anyone else.

Iris got the plates. Grammy filled the glasses with milk. They sat and closed their eyes, and Grammy gave thanks to God for the food. They smiled and picked up their forks, glad for the time they were having together. As they sat at the table, together and alone, the waiting for the warm food was over. Iris sat tall in her chair—for the woman who was with her and the woman she hoped to become. ❉

“Wait an hour to go swimming after you eat or you’ll drown.”

Grandmother—a wonderful mother with lots of practice.

AUTHOR UNKNOWN

Mémère's Economy

BY PHYLLIS MAY CARON GAGNON

"You're walking too fast," my little sister whined.

"We're almost there, Leslie. See, Mémère's house is right over there," I said, pointing.

The sight of the block where Mémère Mitchell lived filled my ten-year-old brain with anticipation. I couldn't wait—fruity nougat squares (just one), a little glass of Moxie, tiny china dishes for a tea party, and a little yellow hen that squatted as she laid white marble eggs.

Leslie held my hand as we crossed Massabesic Street to the great gray building where our grandmother lived. We walked past the first-floor shops, and soon we stood in front of the heavy wooden door that led to the second- and third-floor apartments.

"Well, come on in!" Mémère called from the top of the massive staircase.

The door banged and the hall became dark.

"Fifteen, sixteen, seventeen..." I counted the steps to avoid tripping and finally reached the top landing and my grandmother's hug.

"You must be thirsty," she sympathized. "Come along."

We followed her across the dusty wooden floorboards spanning the immense hallway. Thanks to the narrow light from the transoms above, I recognized the drab-colored door in the far corner.

The contrast upon entering her flat was as sharp as the flood of light from its windows. Mémère's apartment was warm and inviting with its clean, homey smell.

"I saw you coming along through my window," she said. "Sit down in the chair there while I get you a glass of Moxie."

My grandmother joined us at the white-and-chrome table, and I watched her feet hover above the floor like mine. *Mémère understands shortness*, I mused.

As we sipped from the glasses together, my eyes spanned her one-room unit. I noticed the space was divided much as a house or large apartment might be, only without walls. With a glance I identified the entryway, kitchen, reading area, boudoir, and bedroom. The economy was comfortable.

Of course, even this kind of layout must contain some private space, and I scanned the door of Mémère's only closet. It was always closed. Things in there were "not your business," she had often told us. Still, I knew the compartment contained her one winter coat, one pair of overshoes, one umbrella, one Sunday hat, one best dress, and a few everyday dresses.

Four things were noticeably absent from the cozy little retreat. It had no telephone, no television, no bathroom, and no sink. "Mrs. Brown at the other end of the hall lets people use her phone for a nickel," Mémère had told us. She was sure that "TV is a waste of time." And the bathroom right across the hall was shared equally by all tenants.

"Look up at the transom and see if the light is on," my grandma reminded us whenever we needed to use the facility. Far from discouraging my visits, it seemed that the very lack of these conveniences added to my fascination with Mémère's one-room abode.

The gentle woman took out the play china, and Leslie and I amused ourselves for more than an hour. When we grew tired of that, Mémère worked the egg-laying hen for us several times. At last she announced, "Time to go home."

We put away the play dishes as she took her purse from the closet. Mémère always walked us halfway home. Once downstairs we crossed the street to Bill's Corner Store. "Pick out just one candy for the walk home," my grandmother said.

Then we were on the sidewalk again, and the long trek began. Leslie and I didn't mind the prospect that lay ahead of us. We loved walking with Mémère. Her stride was never too long for our little legs. Her intermittent conversation was never above our heads. "I used to walk this street when I was a little girl," she told us yet again as she pointed out places along the way.

As we strolled along, the thrift of words and the pace were as comfortable to me as her single-room dwelling. At the railroad tracks Mémère bent down for a kiss. "I'll watch you walk for a while. Come see me again sometime."

"Bye, Mem. I love you," we replied.

Filled with melancholy, we turned for home. Mémère's lessons in economy have provided me a foundation for peace and satisfaction through the years. Once content as a young sailor's wife in a three-room apartment, now I am equally happy enjoying the view from our lakeside cottage. Waving good-bye that afternoon, I could not have known how my grandmother's legacy of true contentment would become a valuable asset to me in both lean and prosperous times. ❈

"What comes out of your mouth is a reflection of what is in your heart."

Grandmothers are just "antique little girls."

AUTHOR UNKNOWN

Ivory Keys

BY HEATHER BARNES

One snowy Kansas morning in 1928, Grandma, who was only twelve years old at the time, was awakened by the frantic voice of her mother screaming, "Fire!! Get out of the house!" Her father had left water to simmer, and it boiled over into the kerosene stove. The kitchen ignited into a ball of flames that forced everyone to flee in their nightclothes.

My great-grandmother threw possessions out of the windows while my great-grandfather, with the help of his one-armed neighbor, struggled to save the family piano. Pushing with all their strength, they were able to get it out of the burning house. The comfortable little home, where Grandma and her many brothers had played, burned to the ground with a vengeance. As the smoke rose from the ashes, the family piano sat intact in the snowy drift while Grandma sat trembling.

Eight decades have passed since that tragic morning. Today Grandma treasures her family dearly and displays some of her family portraits atop her favorite piece of furniture—an upright player piano. Her love of music might never have developed without the long-ago rescue of that other piano. In fact, Grandma's piano became a significant icon in my life.

At the age of seven, I couldn't wait to visit Grandma's house, plop myself onto the little black wooden piano bench, and turn on the tiny music light above the keyboard. Sitting at the old player piano, I'd watch the ancient yellowed paper, with its intricate pattern of punched-out holes, roll slowly from top to bottom and roll itself up neatly as it went—and all the while I was carefully placing my fingers over the brittle ivory keys in a grand attempt to play each depressed chord. For one entire roll, I was Scott Joplin lost in "Maple Leaf Rag," and then I became Henry Mancini dreamily playing the love theme from *Romeo and Juliet*.

I was much too young to appreciate the fact that this piano had real ivory keys, but those fancy mechanics that made them come to life, while I sat in the lap of its invisible pianist, left me awestruck. With a keen awareness of my innate desire to create music, my grandmother became my piano instructor. So, in Grandma's house, my sense of self began to emerge.

Each visit to Grandma's ended in a rendition of a newly

mastered piano piece—ranging from the simple, repetitious scales that seemed quite boring to "Row, Row, Row Your Boat" to, eventually, "Amazing Grace." Gradually, as my piano skills increased, my awkward preteen years were softened by the satisfying feelings of accomplishment at the keyboard. As I grew older and more comfortable at the piano, my increasing self-confidence grew with the admiration I felt for my grandmother.

One evening, after several years of musical study, I nervously took my place before a foreign piano within the town auditorium. An audience awaited my rendition of Henry Purcell's "Minuet in E Minor." I'd spent hours practicing, perfecting the tempo and mastering the finger placement. But no amount of preparation could ease my fear of that public recital. I had graduated to a new piano teacher whose specialty was classical music. As I eased my fingers onto the proper keys, I glanced over the sea of faces. There, amidst my family members, was Grandma, who I knew wouldn't have missed my piano recital. With a burst of confidence, I felt driven by her presence, and I finished the minuet with a relieved bow to the audience. I could plainly see her proud smile.

Like Grandma, I found learning to read music a real challenge. In later years, both she and I would let too much time pass without regular practice. But when holidays arrived and all the family gathered, we'd return to the piano bench in splendid attempts to churn out old, familiar duets. Grandma would laugh heartily at our errors as I'd gaze, with a smile, at that familiar metronome perched above—the one that had kept time during many arduous lessons of the past.

Standing in the doorway of Grandma's hall closet, I recalled those past holidays around the piano. Now a grown woman, I stood rummaging through old player-piano rolls. The diverse collection included old hymns, Hollywood hits from the thirties, classical pieces, romantic ballads, and holiday favorites. As I pulled one roll out after another, I examined the aging paper. Carefully, I put aside the most appropriate rolls for my wedding reception.

While guests mingled on the patio, the player piano churned out piece after piece. I briefly spied the yellowed paper traveling from one roll to the next and was struck by its endurance. After so many decades, the old piano rolls were showing their age, yet, like my grandmother, they seemed timeless. And on that day, the soft, elegant ivory-satin wedding gown that Grandma had made for me, without using a pattern, was the same soft color as the ivory keys of her old player piano. Again, it was Grandma's house, filled with family pictures, where love flourished and where piano music lifted my spirit.

Today, Grandma is ninety-one years old and still plays her

antique player piano, and I can still manage a few lines of Scott Joplin's "Maple Leaf Rag" on my simple spinet. As she continues to age gracefully, Grandma's love of music remains solid and as contagious to me as it was when I was seven years old. And every holiday I hurry to the little black wooden piano bench where I again sit under the watchful eye of the old metronome. I, too, benefited from her father's rescue of the family piano. You see, Grandma's deep respect and love for music continues to live passionately in me. ❊

“Be yourself.”

Age is opportunity no less
Than youth itself, though in another dress,
And as the evening twilight fades away
The sky is filled with stars, invisible by day.

HENRY WADSWORTH LONGFELLOW

No More Tomorrows

BY LAUREL SEILER BRUNVOLL

I maneuvered around the IV lines and carefully climbed next to my mom as she lay in the rented hospital bed. I settled in close to her body and read a book without really reading it. Our heads were on the same pillow, and our arms intertwined. The closeness was comforting.

The past several weeks had been a blur. Just ten days ago I had watched as she struggled to blow bubbles with my eighteen-month-old son, Joshua. He'd squealed with delight as he tried to grab the clear spheres with his chubby fingers. He kept missing, yet nothing seemed to deter him from trying over and over again.

That single activity wore Mom out for the rest of the day, but she didn't care. Becoming a grandmother had been her main wish since her ovarian cancer diagnosis at the age of forty-seven. She had hardly spent a day apart from Josh after being present at his birth the year before.

Now the only sound in the darkened room was her breathing, fast and forced but in a rhythm. Then I noticed a gap, a space between her breaths. I put down my book and held her hand tightly. Her fingernails were blue. Then I caressed her face and stroked her hair.

"I love you, Mom—I always will," I whispered. "Are you feeling okay? Do you have pain anywhere?"

The nurses had shown us how to give extra doses of morphine from the pump when we sensed her discomfort, especially since she could no longer communicate with us. Her guardians against pain—my dad, my sister, and I—watched her constantly day and night. Thanks to the hospice team, pain medication, and God's grace, her pain remained under control.

I searched her face for any signs of pain, and I continued to stroke her hair. Our last conversation was now only a memory. Was it only three days ago? I gulped down a sob. It was just in time...

While waiting for the pharmacist to fill my mom's prescriptions, I had paced the aisles aimlessly until I glanced at one of her empty pill bottles. The date shocked me—and prompted me to add a home pregnancy test to my other purchases.

Later I cried when I saw the results because I knew my mom was only days away from death. I knelt by her bedside to tell her about this new grandchild growing in my womb. I wasn't prepared for her response.

"That's perfect," she said. "Absolutely perfect."

How could it be perfect? I wondered aloud again. I looked at her. Her pale skin was soft, and her hand was limp in mine.

I wasn't just sad, but angry too. Sad because she would never even get to meet my unborn baby, let alone watch him grow into adulthood. Angry because she was leaving me when I wanted and needed her most. Her lack of bitterness still amazed me. She was content with just knowing the news of this unborn grandchild. She told me about a special letter she had written to Joshua and all her future grandchildren. We were only to read it after her death.

The gap in her breathing happened again. I sensed something different this time and urged my sister to come quickly. Rebecca hurried up the stairs and into the bedroom.

"See?" I asked, nearly choking on the question. "Don't you think her breathing is becoming more labored, like the hospice nurses said it would?"

She, too, climbed into the bed. For several minutes we talked with my mom and reassured her that everything was going to be okay. Slowly, our words became prayers. We prayed for God to ease her transition from death to life. We thanked God for her. We asked for His mercy. We prayed for comfort.

One gasp...and another...then...silence.

My mom died peacefully as Rebecca and I held her between us. Her absence is still painful, but she left a wonderful legacy for her precious grandchildren. Through memories, photos, videos, and her special letter, my mom remains a powerful influence on her grandchildren today. Her written words have an impact on them as they grow up without her. They are aware of their godly heritage and look forward to the day when they will see her in heaven. ❊

"The best sleep you get is before midnight."

Perfect love sometimes does not come until the first grandchild.

WELSH PROVERB

Grandmommy's Love

BY JANE LOUISE NEWHAGEN

Grandmommy lived three houses down the street from my house, and she was my favorite grandparent. Every morning I ran barefoot across the lawns to see her. When I stepped on a bee, she pulled out the stinger and rubbed Campho-Phenique on the sore. In the summer she picked the cherries from the tree in her backyard and made pies. (Daddy said she washed the cherries until they didn't have any taste left. I didn't care. It was the sugary syrup and piecrust that I enjoyed.) In the winter, she swept the sidewalk completely clear of snow—not just the narrow path to her porch, but the wide city sidewalk that ran perpendicular to it. You saw where she thought the neighbors' property ended because that's where she stopped sweeping.

Grandmommy was a lady. She wore soft cotton floral-print dresses in the summer and tailored beige or gray flannel suits with skirts that fell below her knees in the winter. She'd take off the suit jacket when she cooked. She never left the house without her white gloves—cotton for summer, cashmere for winter. And she wore the most wonderful perfume with hints of baby powder and flowers and some kind of spice.

After my brother was born, Mom sent me to

Grandmommy's more often than before. That was just fine with me. There I was the focus of attention, and I was made to feel smart and grown up.

One September morning in particular, the cool, wet grass tickled my bare feet as I danced down the block. Grandmommy met me at the door and gave me a big, sweet-smelling hug. She toweled my feet dry before I crawled up on the damask-upholstered sofa. After reading me two chapters of Winnie the Pooh, she sent me out to play in the backyard with a basket and permission to pick as many hollyhocks as I wanted. We'd make flower dolls after lunch.

My basket was overflowing when she called me in. Steaming tomato soup and a gooey melted-cheese sandwich with the crusts neatly cut from the bread were set out on a crocheted placemat, and a white cloth napkin lay to the left of the plate. I washed my hands and climbed up on my chair. I felt like a princess as I carefully stirred my soup to cool it and scooped the soupspoon away from me the way Grandmommy had taught me. I sipped without slurping and ate my sandwich without playing with the strings of cheese. I could tell she was proud of me.

"Let me get your apple for dessert. When you're finished, we'll make those pretty flower dolls before you take your nap," she said. She took the apple from the refrigerator and removed the cup she'd placed over it to keep it fresh.

I screamed. It was awful! She'd peeled the apple. Didn't she know that I didn't have to have apples peeled for me anymore? I was a big girl now.

"No, thank you," I said firmly. "I don't eat peeled apples anymore."

"But, honey," she replied, "that's my last apple. Go ahead and eat it the way it is."

"No, no, no!" I wailed. "I'm a big girl."

I slid off the chair with a bump and sat in the middle of the floor crying. Grandmommy didn't know it wasn't just the apple. It was the little brother that really bothered me—his vying for the attention I'd always enjoyed; the visitors and presents that focused on him. It all poured out at once as I sat on the polished linoleum floor and cried and cried at the top of my lungs.

"Now, Janie, you've never behaved like this before. It's just an apple. Eat it up," she pleaded. "It's your favorite kind of apple. Next time I won't peel it. I promise."

As far as I was concerned, there was no next time. I wailed louder.

I'd never seen Grandmommy at a loss before. She just watched me and wrung her hands in dismay. I cried even harder until I gasped for breath.

The telephone was in the front hall. She ran to it and pulled it as close to the kitchen as she could so she could see me. I knew she was calling my mother for help. And I knew my mother had taken my baby brother to the pediatrician, so there would be no answer. Suddenly I was enjoying my tantrum. I was in control!

Grandmommy impatiently waited for the rotary dial to circle into position so she could dial the next digit. Finally, she finished dialing and waited as the telephone rang and rang in my empty house. At last she accepted the fact that my mother wasn't going to come to her rescue.

She dropped the heavy black telephone to the floor without bothering to hang up the receiver. She looked at me and calmly said, "Now, that's entirely enough." Then she put her hands under my arms and lifted me up. She carried me to the living room, sat me down next to her on the damask sofa, and hugged me against her soft breasts. I was surrounded by peony-printed cotton, warm flesh, and that mysterious scent she always wore.

I stopped crying. I didn't know if I'd won or lost, and I didn't care because this was perfect peace.

"That's my girl," she said as she stroked my hair and wiped my cheeks with a handkerchief that appeared from nowhere. "That's my good girl."

I closed my eyes to rest. All that crying had been exhausting. I must have fallen asleep, because the next thing I knew, Mom was at the screen door.

"We'll be right there," said Grandmommy. "We were just taking a little nap."

Grandmommy never told my mother about the tantrum, but I knew she didn't forget it, because she never peeled another apple for me. Because of her loyalty and sensitivity, I knew I had a confidante to consult about anything that troubled me—from problems in school to questions about boys, even about that special man who asked me to marry him. Grandmommy was always there with hot soup and a gentle hug, and she was always wearing that haunting scent.

When Grandmommy died, she was so old that I couldn't resent her going. Her life had been long and full, and she had the privilege of dying with dignity like the lady she always was. No one will ever be able to take her place, so when I need that special confidence and respect, I make a pot of tomato soup and a melted-cheese sandwich with the crusts neatly trimmed. I set a place for myself at the kitchen table with that old crocheted placemat and a permanent-press cloth napkin. I scoop the soup away from me the way Grandmommy taught me, and when I'm finished, I give myself a long, loving hug.

I've tried for years to find the special perfume she wore, but I've had no success. Maybe it was a a powder that's fallen from use or a sachet she made herself and kept in her bureau. Never mind. Grandmommy's gift wasn't the food or the hug or the scent. It was the love. And she gave it to me to savor and then to pass on to those around me. ❊

"Everything happens for a reason."

Just about the time a woman
thinks her work is done,
she becomes a grandmother.

EDWARD H. DRESCHNACK

A Colander of Peas

BY CAROLINE TAYLOR

It's a sunny day in June. My sister and I are sitting in the glider on the screen porch while she pretends to help me shell peas. "Remember the time we threw our cereal out the bedroom window?" she asks.

Priscilla's hair is turning gray, and for once I'm delighted that the older sister always gets the experience first. "It's a wonder we never got spanked for that," I reply.

"Grammo must've never told Mommy."

I push a row of peas along the length of the pod until they drop into the colander. "Grammo never knew. I bet some critter gobbled up those cornflakes the minute we shut the window."

"Poor thing. She thought we'd like buttermilk."

"And parsnips."

"And boiled cabbage."

Mouths crimped in disgust, we share a look of mutual loathing. "I bet Mommy found out," says Priscilla. "She had eyes in the back of her head."

"She never ate breakfast with us, remember?"

Priscilla picks up a pea pod and pinches off the end. "Grammo would have told her later."

"Grammo didn't know."

Her eyes narrow as she taps her cheek with a crimson nail. "I suppose you drink buttermilk now."

Her comment makes me laugh. "Nope. Nor do I eat parsnips or boiled cabbage."

"But you do eat peas. You never used to like them."

"That was you."

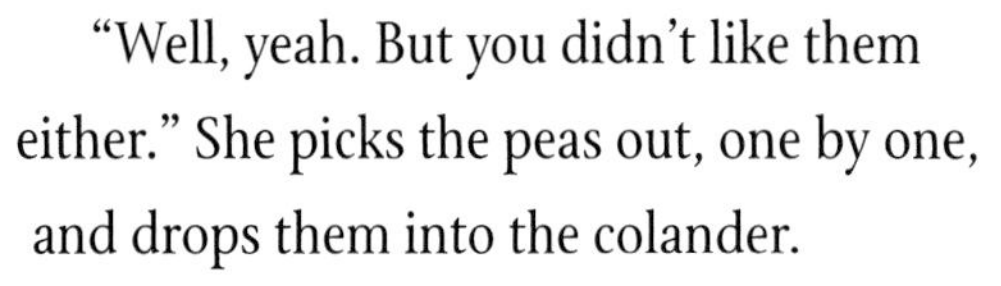

"Well, yeah. But you didn't like them either." She picks the peas out, one by one, and drops them into the colander.

"Did too."

"Not."

"Too."

"Come on, Carrie. I hope Melissa isn't in the kitchen right now. Imagine what she'd think if she could hear us."

I look toward the door leading from the screen porch into the kitchen, but no gangly teenager lurks in the shadows eavesdropping on her mother and aunt. Priscilla's daughter is at the age when anything adults do and say is embarrassing.

"Peas—especially fresh ones like these—are divine," I declare.

"That's not the word I would use." The glider rocks back and forth as Priscilla stands up. She wanders over to the screen door leading out to the deck. "I bet we could eat outside tonight and not get bitten to death."

"If you like," I say.

Priscilla is staring at me. "I could swear you hate peas much as I do—or you used to, anyway."

"No. I love them because you didn't," I say with a tentative smile.

I'm hoping Priscilla's tastes have matured. If not, then that makes me an insensitive clod to be serving peas with our dinner.

"Oh, that old thing. You know it's not true. We didn't always take opposite sides, " I reply.

"I'm sure you've got it wrong, Carrie. Don't you remember that time you shoveled all of your peas onto Grammo's plate while she was away from the table?"

"I wouldn't have done such a stupid thing, Priss. Not with Mommy sitting there."

My sister scratches her forehead as though that will help sharpen ancient memories. "Well, it wasn't me, and I very clearly recall that Grammo divided them up and made me eat half of yours!"

"You are making this up, Priscilla. Anyway, who cares?"

"You always get things wrong. We should write this down so

we won't disagree on it when we get really old and senile."

"Wonderful. The only problem is we don't agree now. Unless... Maybe it happened at lunch? After Mommy got her job at the book depository?"

Priscilla drops into the glider, sending a cascade of empty peapods sliding off the newspaper I'd put in my lap. "Oops," she says, leaning down to pick them up off the floor. "This is such a tedious task. I don't know why you don't just buy frozen."

Because they don't taste the same? No. That's the diplomatic answer. The truth is I like shelling peas. It brings back peaceful memories of my grandmother sitting at the table in the tiny kitchen in our house in Carson City. A plump woman with wispy white hair, she wore half glasses that gave her round, wrinkled face a benign, puzzled look as though she didn't quite understand what was going on but also didn't consider it very important. Decked out in her flowered dress, snow-white apron, and polished black oxfords, she always seemed to be rolling out dough for a pie or trimming green beans or peeling potatoes or carrots that came from the garden out back. It had been a Victory Garden during the war, but my grandparents had pretty much kept tending to it afterward—probably until the day Grandpa died and Grandma decided to move to a nursing home.

A sharp memory surges forward. It's closely tied to the image of my grandmother shelling peas.

I'd dashed in the front door one day to find my mother standing at the telephone. "Oh, darling, please tell me they can't do that!" I'd heard her say as I headed for the kitchen to get a glass of water. "What will we do?"

The conversation went on a bit longer, but out of earshot, because Grammo made me sit down at the table to help her shell peas.

When my mother got off the phone, she came into the kitchen, wringing her hands.

"When's Daddy coming home?" I asked.

Her eyes welled up with tears, and she blinked hard. "Not for another year." She turned to my grandmother. "They've given him an involuntary extension of his tour."

I was too little to understand words like involuntary and extension, but I knew my father was in the army down in Texas somewhere and had been there for such a long time that I had trouble remembering what he looked like.

My mother stood at the kitchen door, her back turned to me. "Whatever will we do?"

"Now, Ruth," said my grandmother, rolling her eyes in my direction. "We'll be fine."

"I suppose I could get a job. Only the girls—"

"Your father and I are still here."

"Are we going to be poor?" I asked my mother.

Her hand flew to her mouth, and I watched a tear escape from her eye and trickle down the side of her nose.

"Ruth," said my grandmother. And my mother turned and left the room.

I remember sitting there as my grandmother kept on shelling peas. The clock ticked in the background while a fly buzzed at the window screen. She didn't seem to be at all fearful or worried. In fact, she was humming a tune as she worked her way through the pile in front of her.

Priscilla puts her foot up on a nearby chair and begins to rock the glider. "This is great, sitting here on the screen porch, doing little domestic chores. It reminds me of when we were kids. So relaxing."

"Do you think I'm a bit like Grammo?" I ask.

Her brow creases. "Are you kidding? She was such a passive creature. Not an ounce of starch in that woman's spine." She pauses to pick at the nail polish on one of her fingers. "Of course, times were different then."

Until this moment, my older sister and I had agreed on at least one thing. Like her, I always thought my mother had run the household and made all the decisions while Grammo hovered in the background, seemingly content to spend her time doing useful things. No starch, huh? Try figuring out how to make a few homegrown vegetables, supplemented by a very small amount of money, feed a family of five.

I pick up the colander full of peas and head for the kitchen, hesitating at the doorway before turning to Priscilla. "You don't have to eat these if you don't want to." ❋

“Be careful...
or your face
will stay
like that.”

You do not really understand something unless you can explain it to your grandmother.

PROVERB

"Me First!"

BY REBECCA WILLMAN GERNON

My classmates rubbed erasers on their test papers until holes appeared, but I had finished my test and was blissfully engrossed in a *Nancy Drew* mystery. The clock above the teacher's desk ticked toward two o'clock.

Less than fifteen minutes until recess, I thought. *I hope it rains so we can't play outside*. Everyone in my sixth-grade class looked forward to playing softball at recess—everyone but me.

At precisely two, the bell rang. We placed our tests on the teacher's desk, and my classmates charged outside for fifteen minutes of freedom. My best friend Judy lingered with me at the water fountain.

Outside, Rick and Deanna, the two best players, declared themselves team captains. After their pronouncement, the rest of the class formed a makeshift lineup so they could pick their teammates. Judy and I reluctantly joined the line.

"Jeff!" Rick called.

"Mary Ann!" Deanna shouted.

Rick and Deanna quickly chose their friends—and the best players. Soon only nine kids were left. I stood glumly beside Judy. Even her company couldn't ease my pain. Then Deanna called,

"Judy!" Seven other names quickly followed.

"Your turn," Rick said.

"No, it isn't," Deanna said. "I just chose Ray."

"You can have the extra player."

"No, I had her last—"

"Are we going to play or not?" someone shouted.

With great effort Rick said, "Rebecca."

Today, like every other day, I was chosen last. Without being told, I trudged to the outfield, the place where I'd do the least amount of damage.

Two innings passed quickly. In the bottom of the third inning, our team was one run behind with only one out. Norm, who could run like the wind, was on third base, and Shirley, who was no slouch, was on second. Recess was almost over. I prayed the bell would ring before I had to bat.

"Strike three. You're out!"

Two outs! Please, let the bell ring.

Jimmy threw his bat behind home plate and grumbled, "It was a ball. I shouldn't be out."

"Batter up!"

I slowly approached the plate. I blinked, and the first pitch shot past me.

"Strike."

"How can that be a strike?" I said. "I didn't move my bat." Strike zone was not in my vocabulary.

The opposition laughed. My teammates groaned.

The next pitch was high. I clutched the bat like a badminton racket and swung it back and forth above my head.

"Strike two!"

"Geez, did you see that?" a boy hollered.

"That's a bat, not a flyswatter, Rebecca," another taunted.

The next pitch was low and outside. I lowered the bat like a croquet mallet and swung. The ball bounced past me.

"Strike three! You're out."

Rrrrrring! Simultaneously, recess, the game—and my life—were over.

"We'd have won if Rebecca weren't on our team," several kids said.

"Next time she's on your team, just forfeit." Laughter surrounded me.

That afternoon as I walked home from school, I prayed that a crack in the sidewalk would swallow me. My heart ached with frustration and embarrassment.

"Mother!" I shouted as I entered our house. Then I

remembered this was her afternoon to work at the library. It would be several hours before she would be home to hear my tale of woe. Whining to my older sisters was pointless; they rarely had any sympathy for their pesky younger sister.

I flopped on my bed and bemoaned my miserable day. *I hate recess. I wish I'd break my leg, and then I'd never have to play softball again.* I sniffed and blinked away tears.

I stared out my bedroom window at the house across the alley. Why hadn't I thought of this before? Grandma lived less than one hundred feet away. She always relished a visit with one of her granddaughters, especially me, her namesake.

I ran across the alley and pulled open the screen door. "Grandma, you home?"

"Yes. I'm trying to hula hoop," she responded.

Normally, Grandma's offbeat responses made me laugh, but today the image of her arthritic body swinging a hula hoop, while she used her cane to keep her balance, didn't budge the scowl off my face. I slouched into a wicker chair and stretched out my legs. A flock of birds could have perched on my bottom lip.

Grandma didn't tolerate poor posture, but today, sensing something more serious was at stake, she ignored my pose.

"How about some bug juice?" she asked.

"Nah."

Even an icy glass of Hawaiian Punch, a treat only Grandma provided, didn't interest me. I folded my arms across my chest. Humph.

"My goodness! If bug juice can't cure your ills, you better tell me what happened."

"Oh, Grandma, it was horrible. I'm always picked last, and today..." For the next fifteen minutes I recounted the events of the softball game and shed the tears I'd held back for three hours. "Why can't I ever be first?"

Grandma pulled a handkerchief smelling of lavender from her pocket and handed it to me.

"Rebecca, I wish I could teach you how to hit the ball so you'd be picked first, but I don't know the first thing about softball. I know you'd like to be first, but sometimes not being first is better." She paused while I blew my nose. "Did I ever tell you the story about my brother Merrill? He always had to be first. Got him into a heap of trouble."

"Really? What happened?" I pulled myself upright.

"My throat's parched. I could use a glass of bug juice to wet my whistle. Do you want one?"

"Sure! I'll get 'em." I hurried to the kitchen and returned with frosty glasses filled with ice and Hawaiian Punch.

After several sips, Grandma said, "When I was a child, we

didn't have all the fine toys you and your sisters have today. We had to make do with what we had. We jumped rope and played kick the can or hide-and-seek. No matter what game we played, Merrill always yelled, 'Me first—or I won't play!' If he wasn't first, he'd sulk and make everyone's life miserable, so he was always first. And I felt just like you did today."

"You did?"

"Yes. I wanted to be first."

"Really?" I stared at Grandma, finding it hard to believe that this tiny, determined woman had ever played second fiddle to anyone.

"One day we kids found an old barrel behind the hardware store and decided to roll down the hill in the barrel."

"I'd probably get sick if I did that. The merry-go-round makes me dizzy," I said.

"You don't see barrels very often today, and if you do, they're made of cardboard or steel. When I was a child, barrels were made of wooden staves and metal hoops. Nails were driven through the hoops and into the staves to hold the barrel together."

Grandma looked thoughtful as she sipped her bug juice and remembered a time long past. I leaned forward, anxious for her to continue.

"As usual, Merrill shouted, 'Me first or I won't play!' and ran to the top of the hill. He waited there while the rest of us pushed the barrel up the hill. I was so mad at Merrill, I decided to go home, but my sister begged me to stay. She said it would be fun."

"Was it?"

"Wait and see. When we got the barrel to the top, Merrill shoved everyone away, climbed inside, and shouted, 'Give me a push!' Evie and I kicked the barrel. It quickly picked up speed and bounced over rocks and small bushes as it rolled down the hill. Merrill was screaming and hollering to beat the band. When the barrel smashed into a horse trough, his wild ride ended, but his screams didn't. We rushed downhill to discover Merrill in a pile of broken staves and covered with blood."

"What had happened to him?"

"As he'd bounced down the hill, the nails driven through the metal hoops had repeatedly pierced his skin. And splinters from the wooden staves were sticking out of him like porcupine quills."

"Did he die?"

"No, but he was mighty sore for some time. We helped him get home, and Mom called the doctor. They laid him on the dining room table. He howled like a stuck pig when the doctor poured alcohol on his wounds. Several of the neighbors, including Mary Alice, the girl he was sweet on, came over to pull out splinters. His bare bottom was on view for God and everybody for hours. I laughed 'til I cried."

"I bet Merrill never begged to be first again after that."

"A smart person would have learned a lesson from this, but Merrill was pigheaded. He didn't change. His me-first attitude made him an unhappy, miserable adult."

"Gosh, that's terrible."

"Yes, it was. But, as I said, a smart person would learn a lesson from this." Grandma waited while I mulled over her statement.

"In other words, if someone wants me to do something dangerous, I shouldn't go first."

"That's true, but in a race with a thousand runners, only one person is first."

I pondered her comment. Questioning her about what she meant was futile. She expected people to think for themselves. I tipped my glass to savor the last drops of bug juice and heard Mother calling me for supper. "I've got to go, Grandma."

She opened her arthritic arms and hugged me good-bye. I was engulfed in Yardley's English Lavender. "Rebecca, you're my first and only namesake."

* * *

Grandma's story didn't erase the pain of being chosen last or help make me a better athlete, but she was right: a smart person could learn something from this story about Merrill. As I matured, I gained wisdom by observing the mistakes of those who went before me, and I didn't repeat them. I learned that being first is not everything. In fact, most of the time it doesn't matter at all. This lesson has saved me hours of stress, disappointment, and aggravation. I never stand in line for hours to buy the first ticket, rush to board the airplane first, or bemoan the fact that others finished ahead of me.

Grandma's story taught me not to dwell on being first, but instead to focus on doing my best. She encouraged me to try new things, enjoy the people around me, and take pride in my achievements. I wish she were alive today so I could listen to another one of her stories while sipping a glass of bug juice. ❊

"When you pray for rain, carry an umbrella."

A grandma's name is little less in love
than is the doting title of a mother.

WILLIAM SHAKESPEARE

Petticoats Too

BY SARAH ELAINE SIMS

"We need petticoats too, Grandma. I saw the pattern at the fabric store yesterday," Anna suggested as she sat on the bed braiding her hairnet out of black cording. Though she was just thirteen years old, Anna's love for Civil War history was contagious.

"Really? No one is supposed to see your underwear anyway, Anna." Grandma guided Margaret where to make the seam. Baby Christian was crying from the back bedroom.

"But they had lots of undergarments, and I saw the pattern that shows how to make them. I want to," Anna whined. "Can't we, please?"

"I can't tie my apron!" Beth interrupted. She threw her apron on the sewing room floor and began to cry.

"Shh, shh, now, don't act like that," Grandma said gently. "I'll help you in just a minute, sweetheart."

Grandma stood next to the sewing table. The sewing machine hummed once more as, with Grandma watching over her shoulder, Margaret sewed another seam in her lavender cotton print.

After two weeks of sewing, Grandma had already finished

two dresses for the youngest cousins. Beth's gray-blue dress had a tiny yellow plaid running through it, and the long sleeves were puffed at the shoulder. Beth had picked out yellow buttons shaped like flowers and butterflies to go down the front to the waist, and a two-tone yellow floral for the sunbonnet and apron. Twirling around to make the long skirt flow out, she let her bonnet and apron go sailing through the air.

Grandma had raised a house full of boys, with snakes, turtles, and crawdads in the living room—and chickens, hamsters, and dogs besides. Camping trips, Cub Scouts, and Little League dominated until at last only her one daughter remained at home. But it wasn't until her grown children made her the grandmother of five girls that we knew what she had been waiting for. When all those girls came to visit at once, Grandma was finally in her element.

"I love it! I love it, Grandma! Can we wear them this Friday?" Joy shouted.

Joy leaped into the sewing room modeling the navy blue print with its tiny purple rosebuds. The dress made her look tall and elegant—if she could just stand still. Tiny white rickrack framed the pewter buttons down the front and edged the high neck and long sleeves. The long skirt would just cover her boots. Her purple sunbonnet and apron set off the rosebuds perfectly.

"If you want to," Grandma replied cautiously. "It's going to be almost one-hundred degrees, and I think you'll get hot in these dresses. Watch out, you're getting too close to the edge here, Margaret."

When Friday morning arrived, Grandma and Grandpa had packed water in ice chests and arranged the three cars necessary to drive to Dallas. Three of their grown children and their families would spend an old-fashioned Fourth of July at Old City Park, a village of historic homes and buildings and a place where they could step back in time for pony rides, cotton candy, and no air conditioning. With Grandma's help, the girls were prepared for their visit to the nineteenth century.

Sisters Joy and Beth danced in circles in the living room. "Mine makes a wider circle," said Joy, spinning around. Her sunbonnet flopped down her back revealing her dark, wedge-cut hair.

"Do you girls have your baskets ready?" Grandma stooped down to pick up Beth's flowers strewn over the floor. "Beth, you've lost your bouquet, honey."

"Oh, Grandma, look!" Beth dropped another rose as she pointed to Anna.

Anna strode confidently into the room, parading the long, bright floral with its white background.

"Anna, you look like you're from *Gone with the Wind*." Grandma stopped picking up flowers long enough to admire Anna.

Anna glided around the couch, stepping over two little cousins playing with blocks. Even they stopped playing to gaze upward. The historic vision created a brief quiet, and for a minute no one but Anna moved. Extending from the bottom of a tight bodice, her skirt swept the floor in a wide circle, and a blue contrasting collar framed her face. Her long brown hair was swept up into the black hairnet, and a wide straw hat shaded her face. Red, white, and blue ribbons circled the crown and streamed down her back. Anna carried a woven basket with nosegays of white silk daisies and blue irises tied neatly to the sides with blue satin ribbon. She gently waved a small painted fan.

"I can't believe you sewed that all by yourself." Grandma smiled radiantly.

Then Margaret giggled quietly and stepped into the living room behind Anna.

"Ohh, Maggie...I love your dress!" Joy ran over to hook arms with Margaret and spun her around too.

Margaret had meticulously braided her long hair and pinned it up on her head. She wore her handmade black hairnet too, as well as a wide-brimmed hat tied under her chin with a white ribbon. Her lavender gown reached the floor and had been finished last, in the wee hours of the night, just in time for the Fourth. Her basket overflowed with white daisies, lilac, and red rosebuds.

"Margaret, your hair looks just perfect," Grandma said loudly over the laughing girls. "And I think your dress turned out wonderful."

Margaret dissolved into giggles and melted into the couch. Then Anna swept past Beth, who had fallen on the floor gazing at her older cousins. Beth just got a glimpse of the petticoats swishing under Anna's skirt. Her blue eyes were round at the pretty lace underthings.

It was time to leave for Dallas.

This July morning in Texas was already stifling in the shade. As the grown-ups unloaded three minivans and seven children at Old City Park, little Christian began to wail against the heat.

"Grandma!" Anna called as she walked across the parking lot.

Grandma was half-inside the Dodge Caravan helping Beth unbuckle.

"Grandma! Grandma, did you know the people in Civil War times would carry their lunch in a basket like this?" Anna held her basket up to the van window. "Can we each carry our lunch in our baskets too?" Anna asked.

Perspiration was already making Grandma's face shiny. Beth complained about her skirt and petticoats getting mussed, but Grandma just handed her own basket of flowers to her. Grandma stood up straight in the bright sunlight and saw the heat from the asphalt rising up in waves.

"Oh, Anna, honey, it's going to be very hot. We're just going to buy our lunch here so we don't have to take it along." Grandma could be very practical.

Despite this and a few historical inaccuracies, the grandmother-granddaughter sewing projects garnered many admiring looks that day among the visitors to this living history village.

The temperature and humidity rose, but none of Grandma's granddaughters complained about her costume. Grandma snapped photos of Beth, whose long braids were poking out of her yellow bonnet, cuddling a lop-eared bunny against her apron; of Joy riding a spotted pony, not exactly side-saddle and her running shoes clearly visible; and of Anna and Margaret next to their father, linked arm in arm in front of a frontier-era frame schoolhouse and discussing pioneer life with a man dressed as a period Native American.

Occasionally, the sight of four young girls in mid-nineteenth-century dresses drew a small crowd that Fourth of July. Surely some sort of historical portrayal was about to happen, folks thought. Though these onlookers were perhaps disappointed, the smiles and giggles were just for Grandma. This was her day. ❊

"Seven days without prayer makes one weak."

Grandchildren are the dots that connect the lines from generation to generation.

LOIS WYSE

On a Journey

BY GRETCHEN LUECKE WALTERS

One of the pleasures of having a red car during a long Minnesota winter is that it stands out against the snow, even in the faint, late-afternoon light. That cold January day I made my way quickly across the parking lot, opened the door, and, after a moment of fumbling with my keys and packages, had the ignition started and the radio humming. I sat for a moment, willing the engine to warm, and noticed a young girl cautiously backing out of her parking spot. On the passenger side an older woman motioned and pointed with her mittened hands. I had to smile, thinking of my own grandma...

We went to St. Paul on vacation shortly after I got my driver's license. I remember walking out behind Grandma's apartment to the row of garages where the powder-blue Maverick slept, waiting for the occasional doctor's appointment or visit from out-of-town relatives. It was summer then, and we were off to have lunch and run errands. Grandma had on her tan, open-toed shoes with the sensible thick heels. She walked holding lightly to my mom's arm, her head and her handbag bobbing as she stepped.

My brother, Hans, raced ahead with the keys, ready to unlock the garage door. After several moments of working the sticky handle up and down, he raised the door and tossed the keys back to my mom.

"How about if we let Gretchen drive?" Mom asked.

I squinted into the dimly lit interior, secretly wondering if I could back the car out of such a tight space.

Grandma cocked her head slightly more to the side and subtly raised her eyebrows. She made a soft click with her tongue, a sound almost imperceptible and classically Grandma. Her strong Scandinavian heritage meant that she rarely directly leveled criticism, but her meaning was clear.

"Well, I don't know. Maybe we should let Hans drive."

"Mom, he's thirteen. He doesn't even have a driver's license."

Another head bob and quiet click of the tongue. "Well, driving just comes naturally to boys."

Needless to say, I did not drive the Maverick that day.

Several years later, when I moved to Minnesota for college, I started making the long bus ride over to Grandma's side of town every couple of weeks. She would cook a simple dinner for the two of us, often Swedish meatballs, some small potatoes, several dinner rolls. These were awkward times at first, but then they became lovely ones. We'd play Scrabble and talk and, having always lived so far apart, learn the things about one another we had not known. I was amazed to find that Grandma had opinions about everything, read the newspaper voraciously, and had a warmth and spiritedness that I had not before known in her.

Finally, as a college student living near Grandma, I would be called upon to drive Grandma wherever she needed to go whenever my uncle or his wife was unavailable. I had no car, so we would use hers, the same infrequently driven, powder-blue Maverick.

"Do you see that car parked over there?" Grandma would ask as I moved the car slowly through the grocery-store lot that adjoined her apartment building. "People sometimes drive too quickly here."

"Yes, Grandma," I would answer.

I tried to have a sense of humor about it, but her apparent lack of faith in me stung a little. Each trip, I followed her directions explicitly and tried hard to impress her with my abilities as a driver.

"You'll take a right out of this lot, then a right on Larpenteur." She opened her pocketbook, took out a tissue, and tucked it into the cuff of her sleeve. "Fine. Now right here, and at the next corner, right again. My, people drive too quickly."

We went on like this until my senior year, when I got my own car, a small red Dodge. After driving St. Paul streets more consistently for several months, I was surprised to realize that Grandma's directions only involved right turns no matter how far out of the way those turns took us. Clearly, she did not trust me to attempt something as perilous as a left turn. I cringed a bit at my own unobservant nature and wondered how different her instructions would have been if my brother or uncle were behind the wheel.

When I picked her up that next Sunday, I decided I would say something in defense of my abilities. She stood at the curb waiting for me, her hair pulled tidily into a perfect twist and both hands clutching the strap of her tasteful navy handbag.

"It's always so nice to see you," she said, as she bent slowly toward the passenger seat.

"It's nice to see you too," I replied absently, more distracted by what I wanted to say than sincere about my opening comment.

Within moments, Grandma started, "Do you remember the way to the restaurant? Turn right here, and then—"

"Grandma, I know, I know. We've been doing this for years." I held my breath for a moment. "And I think I know a better way to go."

Grandma didn't say a word.

As we pulled onto the interstate, I expected Grandma to say something, to remind me to use my signal or to leave three car lengths ahead of me. But she didn't. Instead she smiled often as she looked out the window as the scenery moved steadily by.

When we arrived at the restaurant, several left turns and two highways later, Grandma patted my knee—and left her well-wrinkled hand lingering there an extra moment.

"That's a good way to go. I just don't like driving on the interstate myself. But you, you are a very good driver," she said.

She smoothed her hair a bit self-consciously and looked directly at me. Her strong Scandinavian heritage meant that she rarely directly offered praise. "Of course, sometimes it's just nice to take the longer way."

After that brief trip down memory lane with my precious grandma, I was back in the parking lot on a cold January afternoon, and I watched as the young driver and her mittened companion drove away. With my grandma, I had to earn her trust. It was not a given—and a car ride was a journey, not a trip.

That day as we left the mall, I made a hard right and then another. Several additional right turns followed. It would take an extra fifteen minutes to get home this way, but they would be fifteen minutes full of scenery I rarely noticed—the faded lettering on the awning of the corner drugstore, the church with the magnificent stained-glass window, miles and miles of fresh fallen snow—and fifteen minutes I wished I could again spend driving with Grandma. ❋

It's such a grand thing to be a mother of a mother—
that's why the world calls her grandmother.

AUTHOR UNKNOWN

Grandma's "Crystal Stair"

BY MARITA TEAGUE

When my siblings and I raced down the long hall to my grandmother's room, we often heard sermons on tape. Oral Roberts or some other equally charismatic preacher's voice echoed through the hall. We couldn't wait to see her.

Grandma's smooth pale skin, high cheekbones, and straight jet-black tresses revealed the traces of Cherokee Indian blood flowing through her veins despite her African American heritage. It was her crooked fingers and worn body, though, that told her age as she groped to pull off her large reading glasses.

"Hi, honey!" Grandma said to my father as he kissed her cheek. Then she would say to the five of us grandchildren, "Come give Grandma some sugar."

We each eagerly offered our kisses and hugs, and not long after she would ask, "Grandma's babies want somethin' to eat?"

Any visit to Grandma's always began with her offer of food. My siblings and I desperately wanted to accept, but my father always answered for us, "No, Mama. They're fine."

Upon that response, a composed struggle ensued. She would

sadly say, "Oh, Kenna Jr., you really should let them have some crackers and cheese or a banana or somethin'."

"Mama, no, thank you. They don't need anything." My father would generally pick up a newspaper and casually read through while the five of us visited with her.

She would always ask us, "Whatchu know good to tell Grandma?"

We would talk incessantly, and she always listened intently. Then Grandma, who could never really whisper well, would see that my dad was somewhat distracted and, in a lowered voice, say to us, "You all go back there and get some of those lemon cookies. You look hungry."

"Mama, I told you that they don't need anything!"

"Well, I know, son, but you ought to let them have a little somethin'!"

Most times my father would buckle under Grandma's chiding, and we could then fill ourselves with snacks and goodies beside the old wooden radio in the back corner of her bedroom.

You see, Grandma was confined to her bedroom because of her severe arthritis that crippled her joints and caused her constant pain. Despite that unrelenting pain, Grandma exuded strength, vibrancy, and faith that inspired all who came into contact with her.

Every task she put her hands to was done meticulously, but the years of cleaning homes and being a massage therapist had wreaked havoc on her body. No longer could she make her bed with the precision she was accustomed to. Making her incomparable fried chicken and larger-than-life homemade cakes and pies had become impossible. As her disease progressed, she became nearly immobile.

Managing her long satiny black hair, which she wore in a roll swooped over to the side, proved to be a real challenge for me. Whenever I tried to put in the piece she fondly referred to as the "rat" to roll her hair over, she didn't hesitate to tell me, "Ohhhh, that's not right, baby." After repeated efforts and when she knew I was frustrated, she would release me from the task and lovingly offer, "Thank you, honey. Grandma loves you."

Whether it was wrapping a package, teaching me to crochet, or instructing me how to properly make up a bed, Grandma lived the motto "If you're gonna do something, do it right."

I often think about the times before she was completely bedridden that she struggled to get to church. My sister and I would help her bathe, dress, and powder her face. The process took a couple of hours, but she was determined to press her way to church, and she was always impeccably dressed with matching shoes, purse, and jewelry.

Once during the period of time when my grandma was having a particularly difficult time walking, I had spent the night with her. She woke up determined to make it to church.

Butterflies danced in my stomach as she slowly and deliberately took each step down the treacherous staircase to the main floor of her massive home. I stood in front of her, praying that she wouldn't fall, and then I thanked God as we made it down.

Grandma couldn't drive because of her condition, so we waited for a taxicab. When she got in the cab, I found it difficult to ignore the cabdriver's impatient glare. First, my sister and I had to carefully lift one foot into the car and then the other.

When we got to the church, I went around to open her door, and she would ask, "Okay, baby, ready?"

"Ready, Grandma." I tried to sound confident, but fear often filled my mind. *What if she falls? What if I can't lift her?*

"One," she counted as she rocked her body forward to the best of her ability.

"Two." She rocked again, but this time the rock was steadier and more pronounced.

"Three!" She rocked with all of her strength, and my sister and I pulled her up carefully with as much strength as we could muster.

After Grandma made it to her feet, she held the walker and stood for a few minutes to get her bearings. Beads of sweat fell from my forehead as I anxiously tried to grab Grandma's purse and Bible, determined to avert my eyes from the cabdriver's nasty glare.

"Pull my dress down, baby," Grandma instructed as she smacked her thin lips together to make sure her ruby red lipstick was evenly applied.

Slowly, we made our way into the church, and by the time service ended, I was totally beat. However, the whole process had to start again as we made our way back to her house.

By the time we reached the staircase leading up to her bedroom, I glared at the dimly lit stairwell and grimaced. I could hear Grandma's breathing deepen, a sign that she, too, was tired. On one particular after-church trip, she and I almost made it to the top of the stairs when Grandma fell. She quickly grabbed the handrail, and I grabbed her.

My worst fear came true, and I realized the pain was intense because she hollered out a bit.

"Grandma!" I cried in horror.

Our eyes locked, and she suppressed her pain in an instant, which I now know she did to calm me.

"Grandma's okay, baby. It's okay."

"Are you sure, Grandma?"

"I'm okay."

As a child, I had never realized the strength and patience my grandmother needed to persevere through the obstacles she faced. Racism, sexism, sickness, and trials—she had been a true overcomer on every front. When she couldn't do things for her family that she loved doing—things like cooking or crocheting—she gave us what we really needed: an example of how to respond when life hands you lemons. She developed new ways to show us her love, and she never seemed to look at what she couldn't do, but only at what she could do.

It's been years since Grandma passed away, but she left behind a legacy of love and perseverance that will extend for generations to come. In the poem "Mother to Son," Langston Hughes reminds us that "life ain't been no crystal stair." For Grandma, life wasn't easy. The day she fell going up the stairs, she was still determined to keep living life despite the difficulties. Grandma's love for the Lord motivated her to make the countless trips to church despite her pain. Grandma's love for her family prompted her to often suppress her pain, never wanting to make any of us fearful for her. Life was never easy for Grandma, but she had her "crystal stair." It was her outlook and determination to press up the stairs and through life's obstacles. ❊

“When life gives you lemons, make lemonade.”

What children need most are the essentials that grandparents provide in abundance. They give unconditional love, kindness, patience, humor, comfort, lessons in life. And, most importantly, cookies.

RUDOLPH GIULIANI

Losing Our Marbles

BY JENNIFER DEVLIN

My ten-year-old son Owen loves to have Gramma stay with him whenever I have to attend an afternoon meeting. During one of these recent afternoon sessions, they decided it would be fun to play a game together—and the two quickly found out that what one generation considers a game is much different from another generation's idea. And I discovered when I returned home that their generation gap was more than gaping...

Gramma and Owen were waiting in the kitchen, ready to tell me every detail of their ordeal. You see, Gramma—in her excitement to play with her grandson—pulled out a round metal tin of Chinese checkers. Surely this would be the perfect time to teach him the classic game.

"What's that?" Owen asked her with a sideways glare and a questioning expression.

"Oh, honey, it's a game that my dad used to play with your mom. It's like checkers, but much more colorful—and there's lots more to do. They call it Chinese checkers, but I don't know much more about it than that," Gramma calmly explained. "It'll be fun. Come sit down, and I'll teach you how to play."

She just loved teaching Owen new things and was excited about this adventure.

Well, Owen knew right away that Chinese checkers wasn't the game for him, but this was Gramma...so he sat politely at the table and listened to her instructions. They placed the marbles in their little holders on the tin playing board and then began making their moves. Owen just couldn't get the hang of it. He was trying because he loved Gramma, but this was too much! After what seemed like days of trying to figure out the game, he threw his hands up in the air and gave up.

"I just can't figure this thing out, Gramma! There's no use. I'm not going to play this old game. Forget it!" Owen said with incredible finality in his voice.

Gramma listened carefully to her frustrated grandson.

"I'll tell you what, Gramma. How 'bout let's go into the other room and plug in my video games? I'll teach you the games I like to play. They're much more fun than this old tin and marbles," suggested Owen.

Being the agreeable grandmother that she is, Gramma loaded the marbles back into the tin. *Clink, clink, pop, clink, bang, pop...* The marbles made such a sad and lonely sound as they were dropped back into the tin from generations past. Gramma closed the lid and followed the video-game master into the television room. She gave him a quick hug and graciously loved him in spite of their disconnected interests.

With a game controller in hand and having settled into a comfortable spot on the couch, she was confident she could do this video game thing. At least that's what she thought...

"Gramma, you've got the controller upside down! Hold it like this," Owen said.

He showed her the controller and explained the function of each button.

"Okay, Gramma. Here we go! Get ready to catch some aliens!" Owen said as he flicked the switch, hit the start button, and watched the game begin.

Sitting side by side with her grandson on the couch, moving and swaying as they began punching the buttons, twisting the mini joysticks, and shouting at their enemies displayed on the screen, Gramma came to an important realization: there was no way she would ever be able to figure out this video game.

"What do I do over here? What is that button for? Who is that guy on the screen—and why would I want to jump over him? Can I jump that high? What's the point of this game? What are you doing with your player? Can I do what you're doing? What's that thing on the screen—and why is it chasing me? Does anyone ever win these games anyway? Don't your fingers hurt after a long time of mashing these buttons?"

Gramma's questions were endless, and her effort to understand the game was becoming more pointless with every passing moment.

"Just forget it, Gramma. You are a marble player, and I'm a video game player. I think we better just stick to playing games alone...or at least stick with the board games we both like," Owen said wearily.

Gramma agreed.

They looked at each other, let out a hearty laugh, and put the controllers away. They decided that playing games might not be the best idea and opted to watch a good, old-fashioned cartoon on television instead. The generation gap they had felt during those afternoon hours is one that our culture seems to forget as we live out our relationships at the speed of life.

As Gramma and Owen told me about their mismatched game preferences, I was struck by a very heartwarming thought. No matter what technology gaps there may be between my mom's generation and my son's, there will never be a gap between their love for one another. Gramma will always be one of the most special women on the earth...rattling marble tin and all. ❋

“Eat your vegetables.”

Acknowledgments

Thank you to my literary agent Bill Jensen...for your friendship, encouragement, and help. I'm so glad we get to work together again.

Thank you to my editor Lisa Stilwell...for your guidance, suggestions, and hard work. Your editing touch made a difference.

Thank you to all my contributing writers...for sharing your wonderful grandparent stories. I'm hopeful these accounts will inspire others to preserve and treasure their own family memories.

Thank you to my incredible family—to my loving husband, Steve, and to my awesome, fun-loving sons, Josh and Mike. Your support and encouragement mean more than you'll ever know. I love you!

Most of all, thank You, God, for being an ever-constant presence in my life. I'm hopeful that this book will bring happiness and joy to families everywhere.

If you enjoyed this book, you'll also enjoy

All My Bad Habits I Learned from Grandpa

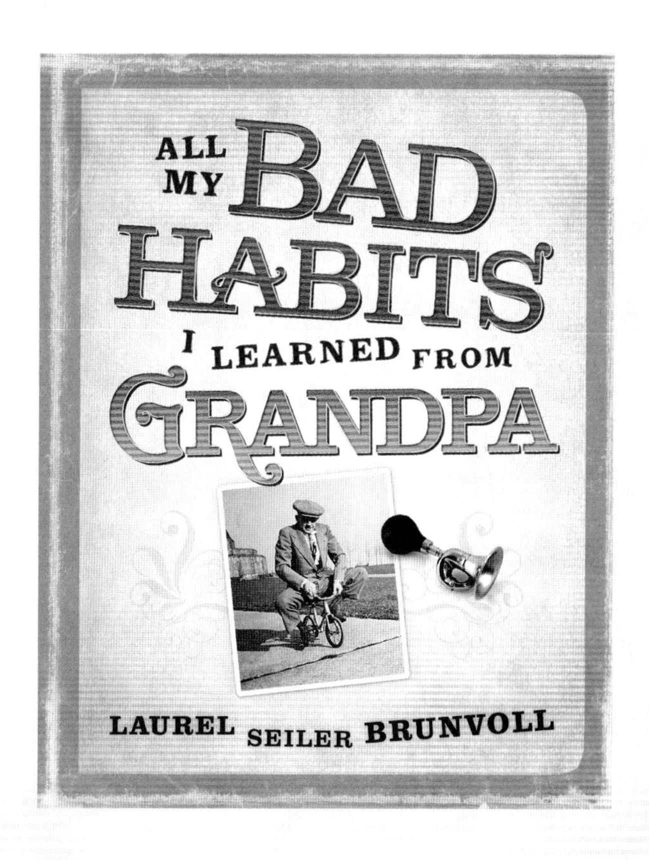